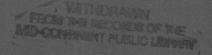

Getting Around

By Train

Cassie Mayer

Heinemann Library
Chicago, Illinois

© 2006 Heinemann Library
a division of Reed Elsevier Inc.
Chicago, Illinois

Customer Service   888–454–2279

Visit our website at www.heinemannlibrary.com

Photo research by Tracy Cummins
Designed by Jo Hinton-Malivoire
Printed and bound in China by South China Printing Company
10 09 08 07 06
10 9 8 7 6 5 4 3 2 1

Library of Congress Cataloging-in-Publication Data
Mayer, Cassie.
  By train / Cassie Mayer.
    p. cm. — (Getting around)
  Includes bibliographical references and index.
  ISBN 1-4034-8392-2 (hc) — ISBN 1-4034-8399-X (pb)
  1. Railroads—Trains—Juvenile literature. 2.
Railroads—Passenger-cars—Juvenile literature. I. Title. II. Series.
  TF148.M39 2006
  385'.2044—dc22

                    2005036561

Acknowledgments
The author and publisher are grateful to the following for permission to reproduce copyright material:
Corbis pp. **4** (Royalty Free), **5** (Svenja-Foto/zefa), **6** (Catherine Karnow), **7** (Colin Garratt/Milepost 92 $\frac{1}{2}$), **8** (John Garrett),
9 (Dave G. Houser), **10** (Colin Garratt/ Milepost 92 $\frac{1}{2}$), **11** (Colin Garratt/Milepost 92 $\frac{1}{2}$), **12** (Jack Fields), **13** (Joseph
Sohm/ChromoSohm Inc), **14** (José Fuste Raga/zefa), **15** (Tom Bean), **16** (Jose Fuste Raga), **17** (James L. Amos), **18**
(Goebel/zefa), **19** (Gerald French), **20** (Munish Sharma/Reuters), **21** (Rick Gomez), **22** (Douglas Peebles), **23** (Colin
Garratt/Milepost 92 $\frac{1}{2}$), **23** (Joseph Sohm/ChromoSohm Inc.), **23** (Jack Fields), **23** (Colin Garratt/Milepost 92 $\frac{1}{2}$).

Cover image of a steam train reproduced with permission of Dave G. Houser/Corbis. Back cover image of an interurban
train reproduced with permission of Svenja-Foto/zefa/Corbis.

Special thanks to Margo Browne for her help with this project.

Contents

Getting Around by Train 4

What Trains Carry 6

How Trains Move 8

Working on Trains 12

Where Trains Go 14

Train Vocabulary 22

Picture Glossary 23

Index 24

Getting Around by Train

Every day people move from place to place.

Some people move by train.

What Trains Carry

Trains carry people.

Trains carry cargo.

How Trains Move

wheel

Trains have wheels.

track

The wheels move on tracks.

Trains have an engine.
An engine can push the train.

An engine can pull the train.

Working on Trains

engineer

A train engineer drives the train.

conductor

A train conductor helps people on board.

13

Where Trains Go

Trains go up mountains.

Trains go along cliffs.

Trains go across cities.

Trains go across the country.

Trains go over bridges.

Trains go through tunnels.

Trains can take you many places.

And trains can
bring you home.

Train Vocabulary

caboose

car

engine

wheel

track

Picture Glossary

 **cargo** a large group of items

 **conductor** the person who helps people on board the train

 **engine** the car that pushes or pulls the train

 **engineer** the person who drives the train

23

Index

cargo, 7

conductor, 13

engine, 10, 11

engineer, 12

track, 9

wheel, 8, 9

Notes to Parents and Teachers

Trains are a form of transportation familiar to children, but how are trains used throughout the world? The photographs in this book expand children's horizons by showing how people move from place to place by train. Some of the locations featured are Maryland (page 17), Delaware (page 13), the Netherlands (page 4), Germany (page 5), Vietnam (page 6), Scotland (pages 8, 9, 18), India (pages 10, 11, 20), Sweden (page 12), Switzerland (page 14), Australia (page 16), and Mexico (page 19).

The text has been chosen with the advice of a literacy expert to enable beginning readers success reading independently or with moderate support. An expert in the field of early childhood social studies education was consulted to ensure developmentally appropriate content.

You can support children's nonfiction literacy skills by helping them use the table of contents, headings, picture glossary, and index.